BestMasters

Springer awards „BestMasters" to the best master's theses which have been completed at renowned universities in Germany, Austria, and Switzerland.

The studies received highest marks and were recommended for publication by supervisors. They address current issues from various fields of research in natural sciences, psychology, technology, and economics.

The series addresses practitioners as well as scientists and, in particular, offers guidance for early stage researchers.

Glena Iten

Impact of Visual Simulations in Statistics

The Role of Interactive Visualizations in Improving Statistical Knowledge

 Springer

Glena Iten
Basel, Switzerland

BestMasters
ISBN 978-3-658-08334-2   ISBN 978-3-658-08335-9 (eBook)
DOI 10.1007/978-3-658-08335-9

Library of Congress Control Number: 2014957152

Springer

Printed on acid-free paper

Springer is a brand of Springer Fachmedien Wiesbaden
Springer Fachmedien Wiesbaden is part of Springer Science+Business Media
(www.springer.com)

Preface

> "Give the pupils something to do, not something to learn; and the doing is of such a nature as to demand thinking; learning naturally results."
>
> John Dewey

During the time of this project I understood one important thing: Learning by actually doing something yourself can enhance deeper thought processes. I think this is especially effective if you experience a conflict, as you never would have guessed what you just have learned. Personally, I think this is a very good approach to discover your own knowledge.

I would like to acknowledge a number of very important people that contributed to and enabled the completion of this master thesis.

Firstly, I must acknowledge my primary supervisor, Silvia Heinz. I will never forget her support, patience and guidance throughout this project. Her ability to ask the right questions and connect me to the right people at the right time led me to the leading ideas of this thesis. I must also thank my secondary supervisor, Professor Klaus Opwis, for being positive and supportive during uncertain times. I would like to thank Dr. Markus Stöcklin for providing very important insights into they ways of teaching and explaining statistics and his patience in developing content text and tasks for the learning environment and the statistical knowledge test. In addition, I want to thank Associate Professor Roland Hübscher for his good ideas, patience and time to develop the learning environment with us. I am very fortunate to have Silvia Heinz, Klaus Opwis, Markus Stöcklin and Roland Hübscheras my supervisors and teachers during my time as a graduate student. Being their student I was able to learn important skills for doing research.

To my boyfriend Cordian Röthlisberger and my friend Satu Binggeli who have reviewed my thesis and supported me when times were not easy. To my family and friends, thank you for all your unconditional support.

Last, but not least, I thank all the motivated students who took the time to participate in my study. I hope they all have learned something new about statistics and their own knowledge. Without them, this study and the further development of the learning tool would not have been possible.

Glena Iten,
October 2014

Table of contents

Tables and figures

1 Introduction

Statistical concepts are abstract and difficult to understand, thus statistical misconceptions can occur frequently among students, researchers and even teachers (Bodemer, Ploetzner, Feuerlein, & Spada, 2004; Castro Sotos et al., 2007; Liu, 2010). These concepts have different sources and occur in different forms. Interpreting results and applying methods accurately are key skills in an academic career. Therefore, well-developed support in learning these concepts is essential for students, researchers and teachers. Furthermore, discovering and resolving statistical misconceptions is also important from a technological perspective. Chance et al. (2007) mention that technical applications explaining difficult statistical concepts are widespread. Programs take over difficult computing processes hence students must learn to understand why and how data are organized and how results should be interpreted. Several research studies (Batanero, Tauber, & Sanchéz, 2005; Belia, Fidler, Williams, & Cumming, 2005; Chance, delMas, & Garfield, 2004; Cumming, Williams, & Fidler, 2004; delMas, Garfield, & Chance, 1999; Finch, 1998; Haller & Krauss, 2002; Jazayeri, Fidler, & Cumming, 2010; Kalinowski, Fidler, & Cumming, 2008; Saldanha & Thompson, 2007; Sedlmeier, 1998; Shaughnessy, & Ciancetta, 2002; Well, Pollatsek, & Boyce, 1990) and reviews (Beyth-Marom, Fidler, & Cumming, 2008; Chance, Ben-Zvi, Garfield, & Medina, 2007; Castro Sotos et al., 2007) present issues around statistical literacy and misconceptions. Some of the empirical reports present positive results of learning intervention in the form of live or online simulation tasks that try to explain statistical concepts on a visual level (Chance et al., 2004; delMas et al., 1999; Lipson, 2002; Shaughnessy & Ciancetta, 2002; Sedlmeier, 1998; Well et al., 1990). However, these interventions only improved some of the most problematic statistical concepts such as distribution types and variation and probability and the p-value. To the author's knowledge there are no studies that have tried to improve understanding of one of the most misunderstood concepts on a visual level: the *p-value*. As a result, this preliminary study developed and investigated an e-learning intervention that tries to improve statistical understanding and reduce misconceptions of students with prior knowledge in statistics on a visual level that will include interactive simulation tasks. The developmental process of this tool included working through e-learning approaches that could be applied to support cognitive processes while learning and understanding in interactive e-learning environment including simulations. It is important to note that the goal of this project is to develop a tutorial that is able to support students having prior basic knowledge in statistics.

2 Theoretical Background

2.1 Statistical misconceptions

Statistical misconceptions are systematic patterns of errors that occur during interpreting, understanding or applying statistical concepts (Castro Sotos, et al., 2007; Liu, 2010). Sources can be ambiguous use of language (Sedlmeier, 1998), inherited intuitions (Sedlmeier, 1998; Watson & Moritz, 2000), and current structure in statistical teaching material (Gliner, Leech, & Morgan, 2002; Haller & Krauss, 2002). There are three characteristics of statistical misconceptions: first, they are difficult to observe (Garfield & Ben-Zvi, 2007), delicate to correct (Garfield & Ben-Zvi, 2007), and they complicate further learning processes (Castro Sotos et al., 2007). For instance, concepts such as the *p-value* can be seemingly plausible but are built on counterintuitive facts and are therefore misunderstood very often and deeply (Kirk, 2001). Bodemer et al. (2004) and Liu (2010) mention that misconceptions occur and hinder learning as fragmented mental representations make the understanding of abstract concepts difficult. This section introduces misconceptions that occurred among students in empirical studies. Statistical misconceptions were observed among understanding of *data distribution* and *variation* (Batanero, Tauber, & Sanchéz, 2005; Chance et al. 2004; Finch, 1998; Jazayeri, Fidler, & Cumming, 2010; Saldanha & Thompson, 2007; Sedlmeier, 1998; Well, Pollatsek, & Boyce, 1990), *statistical significance* in testing (Haller & Krauss, 2002; Kalinowski, Fidler, & Cumming, 2008), and *confidence interval* (Belia, Fidler, Williams, & Cumming, 2005; Cumming, Williams, & Fidler, 2004).

Data distribution and variance. Understanding data and statistics starts with thinking about the distribution of sample data. As there are already several types of distribution to understand data, statistical measures and different characteristics related to these types, students confuse these types, especially if the learning topic is about sampling distribution. There are several interesting studies that have identified and looked more closely into the issue where students misunderstood or mixed up types of distributions (Batanero, Tauber, & Sanchéz, 2005; Chance, delMas & Garfield, 2004; Finch, 1998; Jazayeri, Fidler & Cumming, 2010; Saldanha & Thompson, 2007; Sedlmeier, 1998; Well, Pollatsek, & Boyce, 1990). The most interesting findings and suggestions to improve concepts around distribution and variation were reported in delMas et al.'s (1999) study. They state that understanding representations of frequency and its connection to probability (e.g. in a density distribution) is not intuitive at all because we do not regularly think in terms of huge amounts of data but rather in small samples. They also identified that there are difficulties in several different dimensions of thinking about a problem: application of rules, terminology, confidence (i.e. 'degree of certainty in choices or statements' (Chance et al., 2004, p. 309), and connecting ideas (i.e. integration of concepts). delMas et al. (1999) applied a model called *predict-test-evaluate* to confront students with their misconceptions in a simulation task. They compared this simulation activity to a similar simulation activity without the predict-test-evaluate structure. In the predict-test-evaluate condition, students with misconceptions tested their own hypotheses and created a sampling distribution in a computerized simulation task to test their hypotheses and to confront their understanding. As they received the correct solution, they were asked to reflect on the outcome of their experiment by comparing it to the correct solution. This learning activity of comparison resulted in a large improvement in reasoning and giving correct answers for students in the predict-test-evaluate condition: from 16% of correct reasoning in the pretest up to 72% in the post-test and from 16% in the non predict-test-evaluate structured task to 36% in the predict-test-evaluated structured task.

Statistical significance. Another concept that is difficult to understand and causes a lot of misconceptions is the interpretation and understanding of *statistical significance* (Castro Sotos et al., 2007; Haller & Krauss, 2002; Kalinowski, Fidler, & Cumming, 2008). These studies and the review of Castro Sotos et al. (2007) state that understanding statistical significance is difficult because it is an abstract concept similar to the sampling distribution. In addition, there is another obstacle according to Gigerenzer, Krauss, and Vitouch (2004): the p-value seems to provide the information that a researcher or student really *wants to know*, which is that the p-value indicates the probability for the null hypothesis. They outline that the correct way of thinking of this concept is a counterintuitive way of thinking that has to be remembered every time. Furthermore, Fisher's approach and Neyman and Pearson's approach to the logic of statistical significance are often communicated as one common theory and not clearly separated in educational material (Gigerenzer et al., 2004; Haller and Krauss, 2002). To the authors' knowledge, there are only two attempts to correct this misconception in an empirical study. Kalinowski, Fidler, and Cumming (2008) tried to resolve the p-value misconceptions by using distinctly false applied logical sentences in discussions with students. By doing this, they confronted students with these wrong conceptions and corrected their misconceptions significantly. Another attempt that managed to resolve p-value misconceptions of students by applying a similar strategy to Kalinowski et al. (2008) was the dissertation of Baglin (2013). In both studies, the improvements were on the linguistic level.

Confidence interval. Finally, a concept easily misunderstood is the *confidence interval* (Belia, Fidler, Williams, & Cumming, 2005; Cumming, Williams, & Fidler, 2004; Fidler, 2006). The confidence interval is also related to the understanding of probability and significance. According to the review written by Castro Sotos and colleagues (2007), there are more studies reporting misconceptions among researchers than among students. Fidler (2006) found that psychology and ecology students with prior knowledge in statistics misunderstood the confidence interval as a range of individual scores or that this interval increases with sample size. These misconceptions were mentioned among others such as the confidence interval contains 'plausible values for sample mean' (Fidler, 2006, p. 4) or the '90% CI [is] wider than the 95% CI (for same data)' (Fidler, 2006, p. 5). However, Fidler (2006) also mentioned that by understanding how to interpret the confidence interval, the interpretation of the statistical significance improved. Similarly, Lipson (2002) discovered that the more students embedded and linked the sampling distribution in their statistical concept map, the better was their understanding of statistical inference including p-value and confidence interval. Fidler's (2006) and Lipson's (2002) studies therefore indicate that understanding of some concepts depends on the understanding of other concepts. Thus, connecting concepts could help with remembering and understanding concepts.

Approaches to simulate statistical processes have helped students in applying rules and relating concepts. This resulted in the discovery and correction of some statistical misconceptions (Chance et al., 2004; Jazayeri, Fidler, & Cumming, 2010). Both studies focused on the explanation of the sampling distribution on a visual level, but neither on the *p-value*, nor on the *confidence interval*. Therefore, it would be of interest to simulate processes related to these two statistical concepts. To create an effective statistical learning program with graphical simulations, empirically tested cognitive principles have to be applied.

2.2 Interactive visualized statistical concepts

This section focuses on cognitive principles that have been applied to create online learning tools. According to Rey's (2009) review of theories in e-learning and Moreno and Mayer's (2005) study, there are several learning principles that have to be considered when creating an interactive learning tool such as simulations.

Structure and guidance. In Mayer's cognitive theory of multimedia learning (CTML) (first overview: Mayer & Moreno, 1998), several cognitive processes are described (Mayer, 2005; Moreno & Mayer, 2005). This model includes theoretical attempts such as the cognitive load (Sweller, Van Merriënboer, & Paas, 1998) and Baddeley's working memory model (Baddeley, 1992). According to Mayer (2005), there are three important assumptions that can be derived from the CTLM for the creation of learning material: First, representation of information should be on a verbal as well as on a pictorial level so that information can be processed more deeply in the working memory. Second, a learning person can only process a limited amount of information (Baddeley, 1992; Sweller et al., 1998), hence presented information should be short and clear in a learning environment (Rey, 2009; Sweller, 1994). Third, a learning person has to process information actively in order to acquire a concept in a coherent and meaningful way. Because of his third assumption, Mayer (2005), proposes that information is structured; for instance, in a hierarchical manner where concepts are represented in categories or subcategories. De Jong and van Joolingen (1998) emphasize in their review that *structured simulations* as learning environments were especially effective in the sense that students learned concepts long-term.

Conflict. Limón (2001) postulated another theory that is important in relation to learning environment: the *cognitive conflict theory*. According to Limón (2001), a conceptual change can take place if learners are confronted with correcting information that helps them to reduce confusion. His assumption is that learners are conscious of their understanding of a concept or a relation between two concepts. Next, some new information is presented to them, for example some data that disprove the previous understanding. This causes an uncomfortable feeling and learners will try to reduce this feeling either by adapting the prior understanding of the concept to the encountered information or by stopping the learning process. Therefore, a cognitive conflict can be produced if learners are confronted with their wrong answer or misconception and the correct solution (Jazayeri et al., 2010). To the authors' knowledge, the cognitive conflict theory was applied and could successfully improve students' statistical knowledge in four studies (Jazayeri et al., 2010; Kalinowski et al., 2008; Liu et al., 2010; Baglin, 2013).

Explanatory feedback. The feedback principle in the CTML postulates that the learner should receive not only a correct answer but also an explanation in order to benefit from the learning environment (Mayer, 2005). Similar to general information in the learning material, good explanatory feedback – such as an example solution – should be phrased as clearly and briefly as possible and should be well structured (Mayer, 2005; Rey, 2009; Sweller, 1994). However, as clearly explained and well structured a sample solution is, the task can still be too demanding. Renkl (2005) reported in his study that students could be overwhelmed if a task demands means-end analysis. He explains the process as follows: Means-end analysis is when a learner has to process several steps to reach a goal. Subgoals have to be created and writing the answer increases cognitive load and can reduce cognitive capacity, which results in decreased understanding of the learning material.

Reflection. In a study of Moreno and Mayer (2005), participants – undergraduate students in psychology – selected appropriate characteristics of plants to adapt them to different environments. Moreno and Mayer's (2005) results of their third experiment indicate that an interactive learning task is in general as good as a non-interactive task in improving knowledge of college students, as long as the task was guided and students could reflect correct system-generated answers in comparison to their answers. However, students were worse in answering knowledge questions when the task was interactive compared to when it was not interactive if they could *not* reflect on correct answers provided by the system. According to several studies cited by Moreno and Mayer (2005) (Chi, de Leeuw, Chiu, & La Vancher, 1994; Martin & Pressley, 1991; Willoughby, Waller, Wood, & MacKinnon, 1993; Woloshyn, Paivio, & Pressley, 1994; Wood, Pressley, & Winne, 1990), asking students to reflect about *correct learning content* in texts helped students to understand the content better. The argument goes that reflection initiates deeper cognitive processes such as inference (Seifert, 1993). Therefore, Moreno and Mayer (2005) assume that students integrate and organize old and new information if they are able to reflect about learning content that is correct.

Visualization. Mayer (2011) postulated in his *multimedia instruction hypothesis* that concepts are learned better when using both sensory channels: verbal and pictorial channels instead of just one channel. Corter and Zahner (2007) discovered in their structured interview study that students spontaneously created visual representations in order to understand probability problems. Moreover, to improve statistical misconceptions, attempts with simulation-based tasks worked when students saw how a sampling distribution is built (delMas et al., 1999; Lipson, 2002).

Interactivity. The term interactivity takes a central role in this area of research. Visualizations are interactive when a computer-generated 'series of drawings [...] can be paced by the learner or [...] animation[s] [...] can be stopped and started by the learner' (Mayer, 2011, p. 428), whereas visualizations are non-interactive when the learner only observes them. A study of Schwartz and Martin (2004) found that students could improve understanding of statistical concepts by learning interactively with graphical tools. That was especially the case when their learning context was framed by an experiment where they had to predict outcomes and received more learning resources (a follow-up lecture). In Moreno and Mayer's (2005) study, where students learned about the growth factors of plants in a tutorial, students in the interactive condition selected answers, hence they decided on their own what the best answer might be. In studies about intervention approaches to resolve statistical misconceptions with simulation tasks (delMas et al., 1999), students had to observe simulation processes while changing parameters such as the sample size N were selected for them. In both studies, students had to select answers on their own. Another study that directly compared interactivity to non-interactivity in multimedia learning environment was conducted by Evans and Gibbons (2007) who found that students learning with interactive images and texts outperformed students learning with a non-interactive images and texts. Therefore, interactivity with the learning content seems to have an effect on learning outcome. However, we were specifically interested in what would happen if students selected the parameters on their own. Therefore, in this study 'interactivity' is defined as the process where students take an active part in learning and decide on their own how to interact with a graphical simulation. The cognitive process behind the interactivity is comparable to reflection (Moreno & Mayer, 2005). According to their explanation, in both cognitive processes students have to integrate and organize old and new information in order to make sense of a concept that they want to acquire.

2.3 Improvement in knowledge

The aim of this study was to find out what role interactivity plays in learning with graphical simulations. To reach this goal, the described learning principles and empirical insights were combined to create an interactive e-learning environment in the form of a tutorial in which students could interactively change visualizations and answer questions.

Overall, Moreno and Mayer (2005) discovered that students performed well in knowledge transfer tests if they interacted with a structured program and could reflect on correct answers. Hence the question for this study is whether reflection is enough or whether *interactivity* is needed for deeper cognitive processing and improvement in knowledge and understanding statistics. Therefore we kept the e-learning principles structure and guidance, conflict, explanatory feedback and reflection the same for both test groups. Most importantly, we adapted the structure *predict-test-evaluate* (Chance et a., 2004; delMas et al., 1999) and created tasks where students had to hypothesize how statistical visualizations change when certain parameters are changed. Then the students conducted tests where they set parameters to change the visualization. By creating these kinds of tasks, the principles structure and guidance, and conflict were applied. To investigate the influence of interactivity, we manipulated the way students interacted with visualizations – the statistical graphs. The group that could interact with the graphs was called the *dynamic test group* and the group that could not interact with the graphs was called the *static test group*. This manipulation might reveal whether interactivity is necessary or whether other e-learning principles are enough for a significant increase in statistical knowledge and understanding.

To detect changes in knowledge and understanding, we measured students' statistical knowledge and understanding three times, once before and twice after learning with the tutorial. The increase in knowledge and understanding was measured by questions that demanded knowing not only the definition of a concept but also its application to statistical graphs. Furthermore, the subjective perceived increase in knowledge and understanding was measured.

According to prior stated theoretical insights (delMas et al., 1999; Moreno & Mayer, 2005), the following outcomes in test performance for the experimental groups are expected. It is assumed that the dynamic test group will be supported in their learning process by the live interaction that they are allowed to perform: they can change diagrams by changing parameters related to the concept in order to understand how the concept works. As a result, they should have more cognitive capacity in order to understand how a statistical graph can change. Therefore, participants in the dynamic condition will be better in processing explained concepts in these tasks and will have a higher sum of test score. However, the knowledge and understanding performance should not differ in the pretest because measured prior knowledge is expected to be the same. Hence, the following interaction is expected:

$$(1) \quad \mu_{static\_pretest} = \mu_{dynamic\_pretest},$$
$$but \ \mu_{static\_post\text{-}test1} < \mu_{dynamic\_post\text{-}test1}$$
$$and \ \mu_{static\_post\text{-}test2} < \mu_{dynamic\_post\text{-}test2}$$

Second, in addition to an immediate post-test, a delayed post-test (post-test 2) was included in order to observe performance of retention after some weeks.

This outcome could be interesting because studies about statistical misconceptions observed how concepts were learned over time (Lipson, 2002). The e-learning principles – structure and guidance, conflict, explanatory feedback and reflection – are integrated in both interactive versions of the tutorial, static and dynamic. Therefore we expect an increase in knowledge and understanding in post-test 1 (immediate post-test) and post-test 2 (delayed post-test) compared to pretest:

(2) $\mu_{\text{pretest}} < \mu_{\text{post-test1}}$ and $\mu_{\text{pretest}} < \mu_{\text{post-test2}}$.

The predicted outcomes (1) and (2) are expected for objective as well as for subjective measures.

3 Method

3.1 Experimental design

The experimental design was a 2x3 between-subject factorial design with repeated measures in the second factor. The first factor was represented by the kind of intervention students received while working with the online tutorial. It was called degree of interactivity. Students in the dynamic test group ($n = 21$) were able to interact with statistical graphs using numerical input fields. Students in the static test group 1 ($n = 18$) could only inspect the statistical graphs but could not change the graphs. Further details about the interaction will be explained in the material and apparatus section. The second factor was the time when students were asked about their statistical knowledge: pretest, immediate post-test and delayed post-test.

3.2 Participants

Thirty-nine students from the Department of Psychology, University of Basel participated in our study. Of these, 35 were undergraduate (31) or graduate students (4) in psychology. A majority (38 out of 39) of these students attended the same introductory course in Statistics 1 given by the same teacher. One participant studied economics in a graduate program and had also attended a similar introductory course in statistics for his degree. Of the participants, 30 were female and 9 male, with an average age of 23.64 ($SD = 3.31$, range: 19 - 35) years. These participants think that statistics is rather important for their career ($M = 4.41$, $SD = 1.07$, range: 2 - 6). Their prior knowledge is on average at 4.35 points ($M = 4.35$, $SD = 1.04$, range: 2 to 6).

3.3 Materials and apparatus

For the intervention we developed a prototype of an interactive tutorial called *Statisticum*. This web-based program is written in HTML, JavaScript, and CSS and was created by the authors and programmed by one of our collaborating researchers at the department of human computer interaction. In this tutorial, the student goes through educational texts and tasks that introduce and explain pre-defined statistical concepts step by step. The tutorial content focused on explaining certain statistical concepts: distribution of data, sampling distribution, confidence interval and p-value. Table A in Appendix A displays the goals of tasks in modules 1 to 3 of the online tutorial in order. As the tool needs more time to be developed into a qualitative well-structured learning environment, module 3 was not finished by the time the experiment took place. Hence, participants of this study only worked through modules 1 and 2.

Structure and guidance. To guide students through the learning material, the online tutorial contained two modules each for a main topic. There were questions to focus students' attention to process important concepts (see figure 1, Question → Focus) and relate the concepts to each other. In addition, the content was hierarchically structured so that students could divide knowledge into groups and subgroups (see Appendix A). That is why all tasks were presented to all participants in the same structure. Each module had an introduction at the beginning and a summary at the end. Both modules included knowledge as well as *predict-test-evaluate* tasks (see figure 1). The second kind of tasks were simulation tasks and contained an additional structure in the form of a short experiment, which will be further explained in the paragraph about the operationalization of interactivity.

Explanatory Feedback. For every task participants had to consider what their answer would be. After submitting their answer, they received a solution from the system. To ease information processing of the correct answer, practical examples or background information were added to further explain the correct answer. However, some learning tasks were problem-solving tasks that demanded thinking about mathematical formulation of concepts. To solve these problems, means-end analysis had to be made. Therefore, some tasks had hints that the learner does not have to calculate anything but just should try to reason with what she or he knows about the concept. Also, it was emphasized in the introductory text that students should not worry if they did not know the answer but that they should try to think before submitting their answer. By integrating these hints, we tried to antagonize the cognitive load that Renkl (2005) was talking of when providing general sample solutions in learning environments (see figure 1, Correct solution).

Conflict. In each task, all participants were confronted with the correct solution after giving their answer. After each correct solution, they were asked to compare their own answer to the correct solution. In this way, we tried to initiate a conflict whenever students had to update the concept in their mind (see figure 1, Correct solution → Confrontation).

Reflection. To initiate reflection in this online tutorial after each question participants were asked to indicate within a text box why they thought their answer was not or only partly correct compared to a system-provided correct answer (see figure 1, Reflection). Participants were also motivated to reflect in other parts of the tutorial. In the introduction, they were asked to try finding an answer to every question, no matter how difficult it seemed to them. When there were difficult questions, they received prompts such as certain kind of answer will not be enough to get it right.

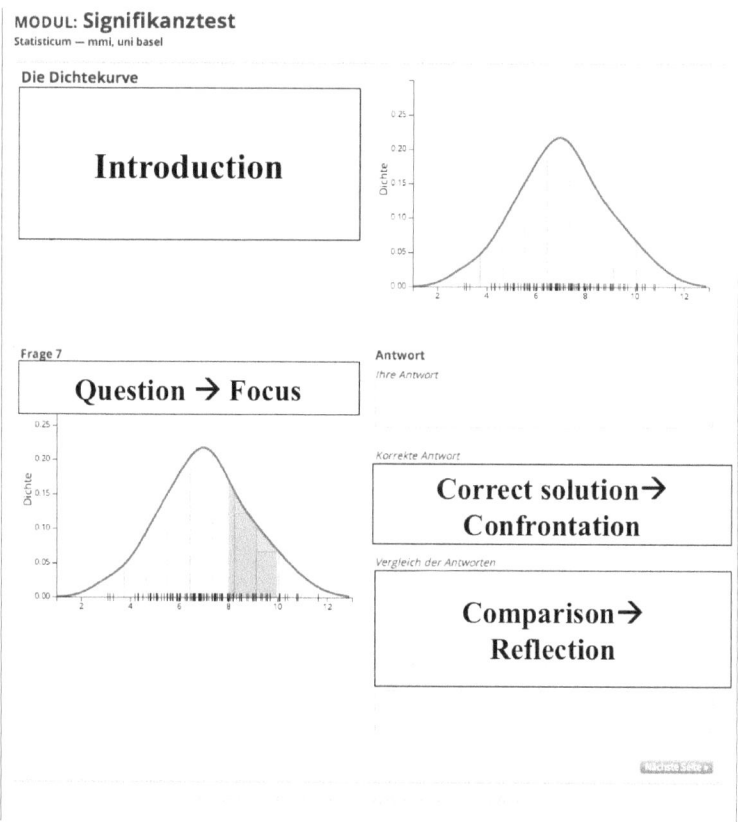

Figure 1: This out-take of the online tutorial Statisticum displays a typical question that represents all tasks in the tutorial in its template form with an introduction, a graph, a question, a text box for an answer, a program solution, evaluation options and an evaluation text box. Students saw a question, answered it, clicked on submit and were thereafter presented with the correct solution.

Interactive visualization. This experiment tried to initiate interactive behavior by integrating a graphical simulation that was either static or dynamic. For both groups, interactivity was embedded in *predict-test-evaluate* tasks. Here Limón's (2001) *cognitive conflict theory* and Chance's et al. (2004) predict-test-evaluate model were applied. This means in these tasks, students had to predict changes in a graph by formulating a hypothesis. In the second step, they had to test their hypothesis and in the third step they had to evaluate their prior-formulated hypothesis by comparing it to the test results. In the static condition, students could not change the simulation by themselves; they were only able to inspect a graph that had been changed for them. Similar to the experiment of Moreno and Mayer (2005), the solution was given to the participants. In that sense, they did not have to consider how exactly they had to change a parameter in order to change a graph. To find the correct answer to the question, they had to imagine how a graph should change if a parameter changes. In the dynamic condition, students were allowed to change the graph of the simulation. Here they had to consider exactly how to change a parameter in order to produce a noticeable change in the graph. Unlike students in the static condition, students in this condition had to master the simulation tool themselves. For both test groups, these tasks focused on one variable, as this was more effective than focusing on changing several variables at once in simulation tasks, as in a study of Kuhn and Dean (2005). Figure 2 displays the steps in the predict-test-evaluate tasks and the different interfaces shown to the static and dynamic test groups. In order to keep learning time equal, the dynamic test group could choose 2 to 3 parameter sizes only. In addition, more than three input fields could motivate students in the dynamic condition to try changing numbers too many times. As a result, some of the participants in this condition could probably lose the focus of the task purpose.

Figure 2: This out-take of the online tutorial displays an example of a predict-test-evaluate task in the static condition (left) and the dynamic condition (right). Black bold frames indicate differences between the e-learning environments.

Finally, to check comprehensibility of the learning tasks and usability of the tutorial interface, a pilot test with 3 students was conducted. These students had attended the course introduction into statistics that was the necessary prior knowledge for this tutorial.

3.4 Measurements

Objective measurements. To observe whether students could increase their knowledge about statistical concepts and whether they fulfilled the learning goals of the tutorial, we created tasks based on the learning goals of the tutorial (see Appendix A). Statistical knowledge was measured on an objective and sub-jective level at three time points as shown in figure 1. In each of 3 sessions students filled out the same 30-minute paper-pencil test so that improvement of knowledge and understanding could be compared based on the same tasks. The test tasks were formulated according to the 7 subgoals of the tutorial (see Appendix A). Corresponding to our tutorial, we asked participants to state reasons for their ideas in some test questions. Here is an example of a task that focuses on the general understanding of the confidence interval: 'A 95% confidence interval is computed to estimate the mean household income for a city. Which of the following values will definitely be within the limits of this confidence interval? (a) The population mean, (b) The sample mean, (c) The standard deviation of the sample mean, (d) None of the above'. We adapted and translated this multiple-choice question from item 2 of the ARTIST Scale: Confidence Intervals, One-Sample (Garfield, delMas, Chance, Poly, & Ooms, 2006). Other tasks demanded predictions of changes in statistical values such as the question 'How does the confidence interval around a sample mean ($\bar{x}$) change (a) if we change a 95%-CI to a 99%-CI? (b) if we increase the sample size? (c) if we increase the distribution of the sample?' (Leonhart, Schornstein, & Lichtenberg, 2004, p. 142). This questionnaire was tested prior to the main study with 3 pilot participants to check comprehensibility of the test items.

The researcher determining the statistical knowledge was not aware of the treatment conditions of each participant, therefore it was a blind coding. Score range was between 0 and 1 point. Some of the test items were expected to be rather difficult to answer. Therefore a 3-level scoring was used to determine statistical knowledge and understanding. For instance we expected test items 3 and 7 to be very difficult (for other item scorings, see scoring table B1 and B2 in Appendix B). Question item 3 had a graph that was very similar to the graph in question item 2. We expected it to be very difficult for participants to see the difference between two concepts (density and relative frequency) if they just compared the graphs of both questions, so we used a 3-level scoring for this question: 0 for totally wrong answers, 0.5 for incomplete answers, 0.5 for correct as in questions item 2, and 1 for correct as in the standard solution. Question item 7 was expected to be difficult because the described situation could have been understood in different ways as we were not sure whether students would understand that the question was about the sampling distribution of the mean. Therefore, we used a 3-level scoring: 0 for a wrong answer no matter what reasons they gave, 0.5 for a correct answer without reasons or with wrong reasons, and 1 for correct answer with correct reasoning.

Subjective measurements. In addition, we assessed students' subjectively perceived confidence in understanding statistical concepts by asking them how confident they felt in knowing and understanding statistical concepts related to the learning goals (see Appendix A). We presented five statements such as 'I think I understand how to interpret the confidence interval correctly.' or 'If a relative frequency histogram is shown to me, I know how to read specific data in the histogram.' and let them rate on a 6-point scale on what level each statement applies to them. Furthermore, we controlled how important statistics is for them in the context of their education in psychology.

Evaluation of the online learning environment. Immediately after the intervention and the immediate post-test, participants rated the learning experience they had with the tutorial. They answered seven questions containing two 6-point scale questions, one 10-point scale question, and four open questions. Participants rated difficulty of the learning content, effort to learn the material and probability to recommend this tool to a colleague who does not understand statistics very well yet. An adapted and translated version of the Net Promoter Score (Reichheld, 2003) was used for the 10-point-scale recommendation, including an open question to give reasons for the rating. At the end participants were asked in open-ended questions about what they liked, disliked and missed and whether they had specific recommendations for this learning program.

Statistical misconceptions. To observe whether students had misconceptions related to the concepts explained in text and questions of the online tutorial, the log file data of the online tutorial session were investigated. The written inputs in answer and reflection text boxes were searched for statistical misconceptions such as misconceptions found in prior research explained in the theoretical background section. Then the concept-specific test item score of participants having misconceptions was compared to the corresponding scores each in immediate and delayed post-test.

3.5 Procedure

First, to control students' level of prior knowledge, they attended a 15- to 30-minute pretest session. Furthermore, measuring the prior knowledge was important: as the tasks in the online tutorial were built on prior knowledge, it was important to know whether participants would be able to understand the content of the tutorial and whether they felt confident about understanding these concepts. In the pretest, participants filled out the paper-pencil test answering the five questions about perceived confidence of their statistical knowledge and the 11 questions to measure their prior knowledge in statistics. Second, between 1 and 3 days after the 30-minute questionnaire, participants attended a session at a computer in our lab where they used the web-based tutorial to learn the statistical concepts. Under controlled conditions, all participants worked with a web browser having the same technical specifications. This session took on average 1 hr 17 min. Groups of 1-12 people were seated at a distance to each other and instructed to work quietly. In order to imitate a normal learning situation, they were allowed to take breaks, drink or eat if necessary. Immediately after the usage of the online tutorial, there was another 15- to 30-minute paper-pencil test with the same 11 statistical knowledge and understanding questions (objective and subjective measures) as in the pretest including a short learning experience evaluation questionnaire. This post-test was completed immediately after the intervention so that we could see what students had learned from the tutorial in the short-term. In a last 15- to 30-minute session at least two weeks after the intervention, they filled out a delayed post-test, again including the same statistical knowledge and understanding questions as in the pretest and immediate post-test. The third measuring time was at least two weeks after the intervention so that we could measure how long the acquired knowledge would last. Figure 3 displays the three measuring time points and the time intervals between the sessions.

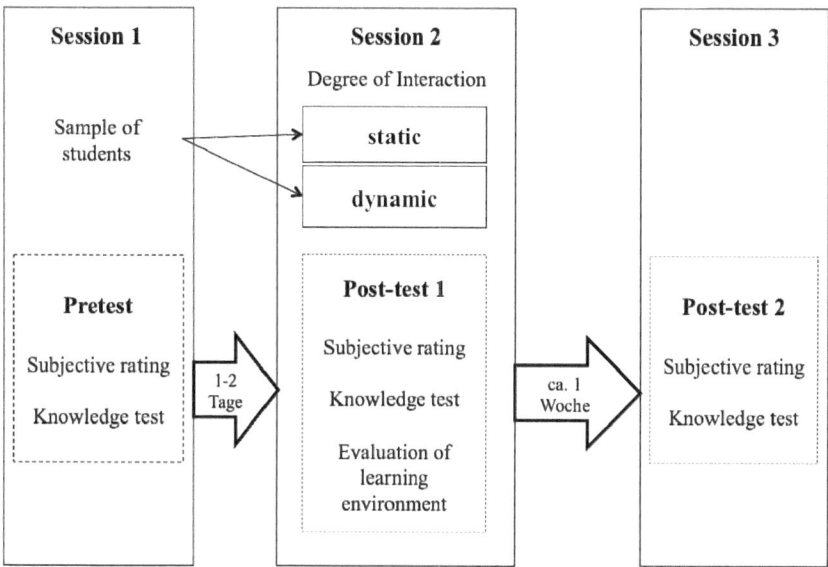

Figure 3: This figure describes the procedure of the experiment.

4 Results

All data were checked to ensure that they met the required conditions for the specific statistical tests and whether they were normally distributed. For statistical testing, an α-level of .05 was used. One participant dropped out after the first session and hence had to be excluded for all statistical analyses.

4.1 Covariates

The following variables were tested for differing influence between the two test groups: prior knowledge in statistics, learning time and attempts to reason during working with the tutorial. The one-way ANOVAs showed that there were no significant differences between the groups for prior knowledge and attempts to reason during working with the tutorial. However, there was a significant group difference for learning time. Furthermore, there was no significant correlation between objective improvement of knowledge and understanding in the test and learning time on the tutorial. In addition, a chi-square test revealed no significant differing distributions of gender, amount of semesters or perceived importance of statistics for educational career between the two test groups.

However, participants using the static version of the tutorial worked longer with the tutorial (M = 1 hr 25 min, SD = 0.37) than those who worked with the dynamic version (M = 1 hr 10 min, SD = 0.26) with $F(1, 37) = 5.24, p = 0.03, f =$ 0.38. Therefore an ANCOVA with learning time as covariate was run to test its influence on the group difference in objective and subjective improvement of statistical knowledge and understanding. The results of this ANCOVA were not significant, for neither objective nor subjective measures.

4.2 Success in learning

Objective measures. Due to technical difficulties, there were missing data points for 16 participants in items 10 and 11 of the pretest. As this could have led to biased means for total test scores, items 10 and 11 had to be excluded from the following analysis. For the following analysis, the sum of test scores from items

1 to 9 were calculated separately for each participant. Of these summed scores, we calculated the means for each group over the three measuring time points. These means and standard deviations for the two experimental groups over all measuring time points are displayed in table 1. According to the descriptive table, the means of the dynamic test group increase more over measuring time point than the means of the static test group.

Table 1: Objective measures – Mean of total sum of score in statistical
           knowledge and understanding

		Measuring time point		
		Pretest	Immediate Post-test	Delayed Post-test
Degree of Interaction	*n*	*M(SD)*	*M(SD)*	*M(SD)*
Dynamic	20	4.35(1.14)	6.08(1.29)	5.33(1.55)
Static	18	4.36(0.98)	5.97(1.42)	5.19(1.36)

Note. Scores ranged from 2 to 6 for the pretest, from 3.5 to 9 for the immediate post-test 1, and from 2.5 to 8.5 for the delayed post-test. The maximal amount of scores that could be achieved was 9 points.

A two-way analysis of variance (ANOVA) was conducted with degree of inter-activity (static and dynamic) in the tutorial as between-subject factor with two levels and measuring time point as within-subject factor with three levels (pre-test, immediate post-test and delayed post-test). The Mauchly's sphericity test has not been violated with $\chi^2(2) = 0.95$, $p = .43$, therefore it is assumed that the variances of the differences between the two groups are equal. Contrary to the first hypothesis, there is no significant interaction effect for objective knowledge and understanding with $F(2, 72) = .05$, $p = .95$, $f = 0.03$. Also contrary to expectations, there is no significant main effect between groups with $F(1, 36) = 0.05$, $p = .82$, $f = 0.03$. However, there is a significant main effect in the factor measuring time point with $F(1, 36) = 25.3$, $p < .001$, $f = 0.83$. Figure 4 displays the significant improvement in objectively measured knowledge and understanding for both groups with standard errors for the means.

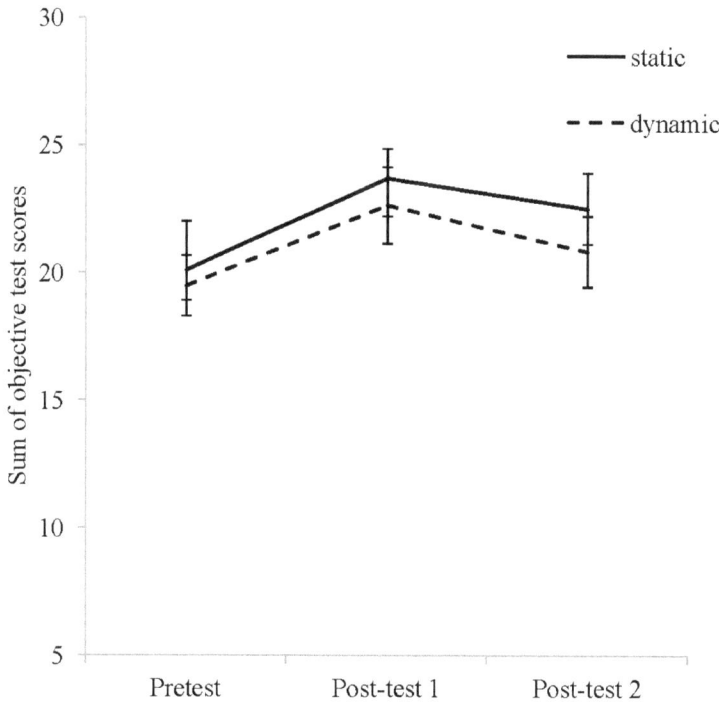

Figure 4: This graphs displays the average sum of objective test scores for knowledge and understanding. Error bars denote the 95%-confidence interval around the mean.

A one-way ANOVA followed the two-way ANOVA to test specific differences in average test scores between the two groups. For this analysis, we calculated the score difference between post-test 1 and pretest for the immediate increase in knowledge and the score difference between post-test 2 and pretest for the delayed increase in knowledge. This ANOVA revealed no significant difference for objective measures of improvement (immediate post-test with M_{static} = 1.61, SD_{static} = 1.69 and $M_{dynamic}$ = 1.64, $SD_{dynamic}$ = 1.40, $F(1, 37)$ = 0.004, p = .95, f = 0.01; delayed post-test with M_{static} = 0.83, SD_{static} = 1.47 and $M_{dynamic}$ = 0.98, $SD_{dynamic}$ = 1.57, $F(1, 36)$ = 0.08, p = .78, f = 0.05).

Inspection of average sum of scores for all test items revealed that items 2, 3, 7, and 10 a) were questions with mean patterns expected as in the hypotheses. Test items 2 and 3 were questions where students had to understand how to read data in a relative frequency histogram and a density histogram. Table C in Appendix C shows these patterns. Test items 7 and 10 a) were questions where students had to predict the influence of changed statistical parameters in distributions.

Subjective measures. For the following analysis, the sums of test scores from items 1 to 5 were calculated for each participant separately. Of these summed scores, we calculated the means for each group over the three measuring time points. These means and standard deviations for the two experimental groups over all measuring time points are displayed in table 2. Looking at the total rating scores, the means of the dynamic test group increase more over time than the means of static test group, although overall the means of the dynamic test group are lower than the means of the static test group.

Table 2: Subjective measures – Mean of total sum of rating score in perceived improvement of statistical knowledge and understanding

		Measuring time point		
		Pretest	Immediate Post-test	Delayed Post-test
Degree of interaction	n	M(SD)	M(SD)	M(SD)
Dynamic	20	19.50(2.72)	22.65(3.41)	20.85(3.18)
Static	17	20.12(4.00)	23.71(2.47)	22.53(2.94)

Note. Rating scores ranged from 14 to 29 for the pretest, from 16 to 30 for the immediate post-test, and from 14 to 27 for the delayed post-test. The maximal amount of rating scores that could be achieved was 30 points.

As the Mauchly's sphericity test has not been violated for subjective measures ($\chi^2(2)$= 0.99, p = .79), it can be assumed that the variances of the differences between groups are equal. Because there were two missing data points, two participants had to be excluded from this analysis. The two-way ANOVA with repeated measures revealed no significant interaction effect $F(2, 70)$ = .53, p = .59, f = 0.12. Furthermore, there is no main effect for the subjective improvement between groups $F(1, 35)$ = 1.73, p = .20, f = 0.23. However, there is a significant main effect in the factor measuring time with $F(2, 70)$ = 21.02, $p < .001$, f = 0.78. Figure 5 reveals the significant effects for subjective rated improvement over time that is statistically equal compared between the two test groups.

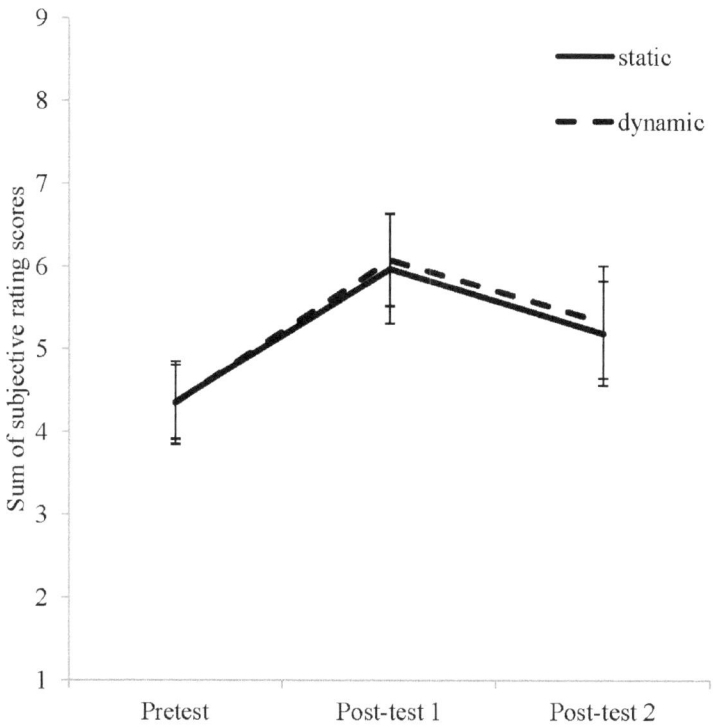

Figure 5: This graph displays the average sum of rating scores for subjectively perceived knowledge and understanding. Error bars denote the 95%-confidence interval around the means.

A one-way ANOVA was conducted to test specific differences in average test scores between the two groups. For this analysis, we calculated the subjective rating difference between post-test 1 and pretest for the immediate perceived increase in knowledge and the subjective rating difference between post-test 2 and pretest for the delayed perceived increase in knowledge. This ANOVA revealed no significant difference for subjective measure (immediate post-test with $M_{static} = 3.44$, $SD_{static} = 3.18$ and $M_{dynamic} = 3.00$, $SD_{dynamic} = 3.33$, $F(1, 37) = 0.18$, $p = .67$, $f = 0.07$; delayed post-test with $M_{static} = 2.41$, $SD_{static} = 3.83$ and $M_{dynamic} = 1.35$, $SD_{dynamic} = 2.50$, $F(1, 35) = 1.03$, $p = .32$, $f = 0.17$).

4.3 Statistical misconceptions

Existing research has shown that especially the concept of probability is abstract and difficult to understand. Therefore a qualitative analysis was conducted to see whether there were misconceptions around probability. There were two concepts that were most often misunderstood while participants learned with the tutorial. Of 39 participants, 31 (static: $n = 17$ of 18; dynamic: $n = 14$ of 21) had misconceptions about the confidence interval in different forms. Eleven (static: $n = 7$; dynamic: $n = 4$) of those who had misconceptions had higher test scores in test tasks of immediate and delayed post-test corresponding to the learning task in the tutorial. Twelve participants (static: $n = 4$; dynamic: $n = 8$) had higher test scores in the corresponding tasks of the immediate post-test only.

The second concept that was difficult to understand was the relation between density, relative frequency and the area representing probability for occurring data in a density histogram or density distribution. Nineteen of 39 participants had misconceptions about the relations between these three concepts. After learning with the tutorial, 7 participants (static: $n = 3$; dynamic: $n = 4$) had higher test scores in test tasks of immediate and delayed post-test corresponding to the learning task in the tutorial. Nine participants (static: $n = 5$, dynamic: $n = 4$) had higher test scores in the immediate post-test in these test tasks but forgot what they had learned by the time of the delayed post-test.

4.4 Evaluation of the online learning environment

In the following analysis we looked at frequency and means of the difficulty and recommendation rating. Ratings concerning effort to learn were excluded because the word for effort in German is not exclusively related to cognitive processing in relation to its meaning. Sixteen participants (static: $n = 8$; dynamic: $n = 8$) perceived the tasks of the tutorial in general as difficult, whereas 23 participants (static: $n = 10$; dynamic; $n = 13$) perceived them mostly as rather easy. The mean was $M = 3.74$ with a standard deviation of $SD = 1.74$ (see figure 7). Whereas 9 of 39 participants stated in open questions that some tasks were difficult to understand, 6 of 39 participants stated that the tasks were well explained and understandable. However, this could be confounded with the perceived difficulty of statistics as a subject. Therefore, we looked closer at the open questions to identify the reasons they gave these difficulty ratings and to find out where the tutorial needed improvement to help them learn the material much better.

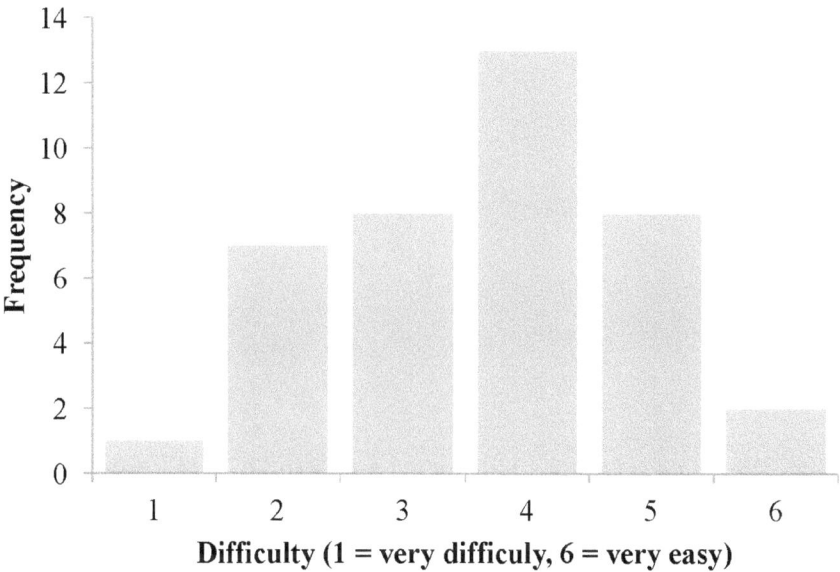

Figure 6: This bar chart displays the rating by students (frequency) of the perceived difficulty of the learning tasks in the online tutorial Statisticum.

A qualitative analysis revealed that the most wished-for changes were: First, 9 of 39 participants wished more definitions immediately displayed when needed. Second, 9 of 39 participants wished back-buttons or other navigation options to repeat content they have previously read. Third, 6 of 39 participants wished more practice examples that would support understanding of the tasks and the explained theories.

Finally, students thought it is rather probable that they would recommend *Statisticum* to a colleague who wanted to learn more about statistics (M = 7.21, SD = 2.09, range: 1 to 10, modus = 8). Here, it is important to note that there were no significant correlations between objective improvement of knowledge and understanding and recommendation of the online tutorial.

5 Discussion

This study investigated whether interactive statistical visualizations have a positive effect on learning statistical concepts. The main goal was to find out whether learning with dynamic changeable visualizations could be more advantageous for students in comparison to learning with static visualizations. A subgoal was to explore whether students can resolve statistical misconceptions.

Effect of interactivity. Against expectation of the first hypothesis, students did not learn significantly more by using a dynamic interactive visualization, in comparison to using static visualizations in a structured learning environment. This accounts for objective as well as subjective measures. On the one hand, this finding confirms the results of the third experiment of Moreno and Mayer (2005), where students in interactive condition were equally good as the students in the non-interactive condition. In this and in Moreno and Mayer's (2005) experiment, both groups were allowed to reflect on correct answers provided by the system. However, another study conducted by Evans and Gibbons (2007) found students can profit from interactive e-learning environments more than from non-interactive ones. A possible reason might be that the study of Evans and Gibbons (2007) did not prompt students to reflect directly on learning content, nor did they add any guidance or conflict to the interactive interface. They only asked students to reflect on learning material in the pretest. Taken together, this could indicate that if learning principles are combined with interactivity these principles can take over the effect of interactivity and help students to process learning content. Moreno and Mayer (2005) have already pointed out that reflection – similar to interactivity – could initiate deeper cognitive processing. Therefore it would be of interest as to how the effect of interactivity could be detected. One option to detect is to *increase the degree of interactivity* as the manipulating factor. For some reason, the chosen degree of interactivity did not help improve knowledge and understanding. First, in this study several topics were presented in the online tutorial and hence in the knowledge test, whereas in Evans and Gibbons' (2007) the same topic was presented repeatedly to the students in a shorter session which demands less cognitive capacity. As a result, students in Evans and Gibbons (2007) study could learn with more cognitive capacity, whereas in this study the tasks were never repeated and hence allowing students to do a task again would give them a greater chance to remember content. As a result, they could increase their knowledge and understanding scores. The sub-section on future research will deal with this subject more elaborately.

Furthermore, the test of this study included only 11 items for about 7 different topics of which 9 could be used for the objective measurements. In addition, 5 items asked about the perceived confidence in understanding 5 different concepts. The questionnaire of Moreno and Mayer (2005) that was used in the study of Evans and Gibbons (2007) had 12 items for 1 topic. This heterogeneous measuring is very likely to be unreliable and hence could have caused undetected differences in scores among students. Thus, another option to detect the effect of interactivity is to *adapt the knowledge and understanding test tasks*. Interestingly, according to descriptive data (see means in table 2 and 3), the dynamic test group seemed to improve more over time than the static test group in objective test scores. Some test tasks were sensitive for these expected patterns of mean differences (see Appendix C, items 2, 3, 7 and 10 a)). This descriptive finding is similar to the descriptive finding of Moreno and Mayer (2005) in the third experiment. Students in the interactive condition of their study were especially good in close and distant transfer tasks. This could indicate that certain types of questions are more sensitive to the effect of interactivity on learning. For instance, two items demanded predictions (items 7 and 10 a)) or a practical approach to a problem (items 2 and 3). Moreover, Evans and Gibbons (2007) and Moreno and Mayer (2005) were able to show the effect of interactivity by applying adapted transfer questions.

Improvement over time. Because Lipson (2002) stated that it is important to observe development of conceptual knowledge over time, we looked at improvement of knowledge and understanding statistics after a specific period of time. As expected in the second hypothesis, this study indicates that students were able to profit from the tutorial long-term. Students in both test groups significantly improved knowledge and understanding in statistics from pretest to immediate and delayed post-test (see figure 5 and 6). The observed improvements occurred for objective as well as for subjective measures. In this case, the effect sizes were large ($f = 0.83$ for objective, $f = 0.76$ for subjective measures). Lipson (2002) was able to show similar improvements with his study about interactive tasks with concept maps, where students had to connect statistical concepts to each other. However, only some students were able to profit from this intervention and increase their statistical knowledge long-term. A reason for this might be that statistical concepts are complex and difficult to remember. Another study (Hulshof, Eysink, Loyens, & de Jong, 2005) testing interactivity found improved knowledge in the delayed post-test but not in the immediate post-test. Therefore, it might be hypothesized that the effect of interactivity needs time to be revealed.

Together with the results from the first hypothesis, this means students in both test groups experienced a comparable improvement in statistical concept knowledge and understanding after working with the online tutorial.

Explorative results. Besides the planned and tested investigation of hypotheses in this study, other effects were explored. Many students had misconceptions about either the confidence interval or the probability in relation to the relative frequency and the density during working with the online tutorial. Both are well known to be difficult concepts that are often misunderstood among students (Bodemer et al., 2004; Castro Sotos, et al. 2007; Liu, 2010). In this study, misconceptions around probability could be observed similar to the study of Shaughnessy and Ciancetta (2002), who found these probability misconceptions among students. In addition, we found misconceptions around the confidence interval, as did Fidler (2006). Just like students in Fidler's (2006) study, the students of this study often misunderstood that the confidence interval is a range of individual scores. Another misconception that was observed among researchers (Belia, Fidler, Williams, & Cumming, 2005; Cumming, Williams, & Fidler, 2004) was that they expected the intervals to be at more or less the same position in a simulation of repeated randomized sampling. This could also be observed in this study too. However, it was possible for a majority of students with misconceptions to improve conceptual understanding after the tutorial. Over all test groups, the tutorial might have intervened with explanatory feedback so that students could improve their understanding of the confidence interval or the probability. A limiting factor to this finding might be that the length of the tutorial session could have increased cognitive capacity. This might have caused decreased cognitive processing of learning tasks and misconceptions could have occurred more easily. This is assumed because some students expressed concerns about being too tired to concentrate in the open evaluation questions. Moreover, most students rated the learning tasks about probability and confidence interval concepts as very difficult to understand or solve. It is likely that fewer misconceptions might have occurred under easier learning circumstances. In addition, it is not certain that the actual misconceptions were resolved, as we did not interview the students, in contrast to the study of Chance et al. (2004).

5.1 Limitations

The a major assumption of this study was that students in the dynamic condition would think about the relationship between the changing parameter and the distribution in a more precise way compared to the students in the static condition. It might have been that the dynamic test group had to think more about how to test with usable numbers while they changed the graphs interactively. As a result, cognitive load to process given information was too high in the dynamic test group to have an advantage in learning statistical concepts over the static group. Because of the higher demand it might have been that the test parts of the predict-test-evaluate learning tasks were too tempting for students in the dynamic condition to skip deep cognitive processing and just try numbers that were not thought through or planned ahead. Some students used unreasonably high numbers or numbers that did not differ much from a second number such as sample sizes of 2 and 10. This might indicate a passive learning behavior as Ainsworth (1999) argued in her review about dynamically linked representations. However, how much effort they had put in each preparation of the test in the predict-test-evaluate task was not controlled. The only way it could be inferred in such a study is by investigating time working with a predict-test-evaluate task together with the amount of reasoning they put into these tasks and the reasonable numbers they have used to test in the dynamic conditions. Furthermore, of these measures only amount of reasoning and time working in predict-test-evaluate tasks could be compared between groups. These measures were not significantly different between the test groups.

Moreover, the unnatural setting of the learning intervention reduces the external validity of the results. Students were allowed to take learning breaks but almost all of them worked through the session without leaving their seat. On the other hand, this enabled a controlled experimental setting. Finally, the qualitative analysis revealed that two tasks in the tutorial were too difficult for most students to understand and solve. In further studies, these tasks must be made easier for the majority of students, otherwise the cognitive load and the subjectively perceived confidence about knowledge and understanding could lead to a lower compliance rate or a floor effect in measurements of these variables.

5.2 Future research

A major implication was that we did not control the effort the students in the dynamic condition put into testing parameters in the tutorial. By controlling this, it might be more probable to observe whether students integrate and organize new information and process information deeply. A possibility to do this would be to ask students while learning with the tutorial to provide short notes in a text box in order to show what numbers for parameters they plan to choose for testing and why. Consequentially, to analyze these answers, a way should be found to categorize the quality of observed reasons and hypotheses. Providing the option to repeat testing in dynamic predict-test-evaluate tasks could also increase interactivity, because Moreno and Mayer (2005) and Evans and Gibbons (2007) let students repeatedly exercise interactive tasks until they learned the principle successfully. There is another study that applied repetition in dynamic visualization tasks successfully (Trey & Kahn, 2008). The authors' guidance principle GEM (generate/evaluate/modify) is comparable to the predict-test-evaluate model (Chance et al., 2004).

Renkl (2005) mentioned that sample solutions can be cognitively demanding if they include several steps to solve the problem. Moreover, some participants wished for more support by examples that explain system-provided solutions. Therefore, providing a sample solution was another factor that might have influenced students' performance in this study. According to Renkl (2013), this could be very intriguing to observe as the body of research done in this area is huge and often supports that learning with examples is effective (Salden, Koedinger, Renkl, Aleven, & McLaren, 2010). There seems to be a huge potential to test ways to present solutions to students. For instance, solutions must be presented in easily understandable ways to ensure that the students' cognitive process is focused on the task and not on the understanding of the solution (Rey, 2009).

Besides the small sample size, participants coming from different semesters of psychology might have caused knowledge differences among students that were not detected by the newly developed short knowledge and understanding test. For further studies, a larger total sample size of at least 100 participants should be considered to increase test power. This would also have the advantage of allowing an item analysis of our knowledge and understanding test.

It is very likely that the heterogeneous knowledge and understanding test was unreliable and could not detect differences due to interactivity. Increasing the amount of items for knowledge and understanding could increase the reliability of the whole test, which could lead to a more exact detection of differences in knowledge and understanding between groups. In addition, students in the dynamic test group of this study were often better in reasoning tasks where they had to reason about learned concepts of the tutorial. It can be assumed that they transferred knowledge. Moreover, Moreno, and Mayer (2005) asked transfer questions where students in their dynamic test group were especially good in terms of scores. Therefore, it will be of interest to increase reliability of these primal tested items that demanded reasoning. In order to measure knowledge and understanding more exactly, more items should be developed to ask about principles corresponding to the predict-test-evaluate tasks in the tutorial. These items should measure knowledge that can only be transferred if participants have thought about testing with real numbers before. There is one other important suggestion for a change of the knowledge and understanding test. The causation of misconceptions and improvement of such difficult concepts must be inspected in detail, as misconceptions have been discovered in detailed investigations such as clinical interviews with open-ended questions (Chance et al., 2004). In an experimental setting such as here, this could be achieved with open-ended questions explicitly demanding definitions of these concepts.

5.3 Conclusion

Students were able to improve knowledge and understanding of statistics when the intervention was structured, confronted them with knowledge gaps and provided explanatory feedback. However, as there was no significant interaction effect but a learning effect over time, students were equally good considering observed improvements in objective as well as subjective measures. To understand how a higher degree of interactivity could positively influence success in learning, a follow-up study should include a more sensitive knowledge test with a higher power and simulation learning tasks integrated in a more interactive e-learning environment.

References

Ainsworth, S. (1999). The functions of multiple representations. *Computers & Education, 33*(2), 131-152. Retrieved from: http://www.compassproject.net/sadhana/ teaching/ readings/ainsworth.pdf

Baddeley, A. D. (1992). Working memory. *Science, 255,* 556-559. Retrieved from: http:// www2.psych.ubc.ca/~pgraf/Psy583Readings/Baddeley%201983.pdf

Baglin, J. (2013). *Evaluating Learning Theory-based Methods for Improving the Learning Outcomes of Introductory Statistics Courses* Unpublished Doctoral dissertation, RMIT University. Retrieved from: http://researchbank.rmit.edu.au/eserv/rmit: 160411/Baglin.pdf

Batanero, C., Tauber, L. M., & Sánchez, V. (2004). Students' reasoning about the normal distribution. *The challenge of developing statistical literacy, reasoning, and thinking, 257-276. Retrieved from: http://www.researchgate.net/publication/226052237 _Reasoning_about_Data_Analysis/file/d912f50c5acba63b24.pdf#page=262

Belia, S., Fidler, F., Williams, J., & Cumming, G. (2005). Researchers misunderstand confidence intervals and standard error bars. *Psychological methods, 10*(4), 389. doi: 10.1037/1082-989X.10.4.389

Beyth-Marom, R., Fidler, F., & Cumming, G. (2008). Statistical cognition: Towards evidence-based practice in statistics and statistics education. *Statistics Education Research Journal, 7*(2), 20-39. Retrieved from: Bhttps://www.stat.auckland.ac.nz/ ~iase/serj/SERJ7(2)_Beyth-Maron.pdf

Bodemer, D., Ploetzner, R., Feuerlein, I., & Spada, H. (2004). The active integration of information during learning with dynamic and interactive visualisations. *Learning and Instruction, 14*(3), 325-341. doi:10.1016/j.learninstruc.2004.06.006

Castro Sotos, A. E., Vanhoof, S., Van den Noortgate, W., & Onghena, P. (2007). Students' misconceptions of statistical inference: A review of the empirical evidence from research on statistics education. *Educational Research Review, 2*(2), 98-113. doi:10.1016/j.edurev.2007.04.001

Chance, B., delMas, R., & Garfield, J. (2004). Reasoning about Sampling Distributions. *The challenge of developing statistical literacy, reasoning and thinking, 295-323. Retrieved from: http://www.researchgate.net/publication/226718118_Research_ on_Statistical_Literacy_Reasoning_and_Thinking_Issues_Challenges_and_Implicat ions/file/d912f50c5acba0b7b9.pdf

Chance, B., Ben-Zvi, Garfield, & Medina (2007). The role of technology in improving student learning of statistics. *Technology Innovations in Statistics Education Journal 1*(1), 1-24. Retrieved from: http://sites.google.com/site/danibenzvi/TISETheRole ofTechnologyTISE2007.pdf

Chi, M. T., De Leeuw, N., Chiu, M. H., & LaVancher, C. (1994). Eliciting self-explanations improves understanding. *Cognitive science*, *18*(3), 439-477. Retrieved from: http:// www.public.asu.edu/~mtchi/papers/Self-explanations94.pdf

Corter, J. E., & Zahner, D. C. (2007). Use of external visual representations in probability problem solving. *Statistics Education Research Journal*, *6*(1), 22-50. Retrieved from: http://www.stat.auckland.ac.nz/~iase/serj/SERJ6(1)_Corter_Zahner.pdf

Cumming, G., Williams, J., & Fidler, F. (2004). Replication and researchers' understanding of confidence intervals and standard error bars. *Understanding Statistics*, *3*(4), 299-311. doi: 10.1207/s15328031us0304_5

de Jong, T., & van Joolingen, W. R. (1998). Scientific Discovery Learning With Computer Simulations of Conceptual Domains. *Review of Educational Research*, *68*(2), 179-201. Retrieved from: http://hal.archives-ouvertes.fr/docs/00/19/06/80/PDF/de Jong-Ton-1998b.pdf

delMas, R.C., Garfield, J., & Chance, B.L. (1999). A Model of Classroom Research in Action: Developing Simulation Activities to Improve Students' Statistical Reasoning. *Journal of Statistics Education*, *7*(3). Retrieved form: http://www.amstat.org/publications/jse/secure/v7n3/delmas.cfm

Evans, C., & Gibbons, N. J. (2007). The interactivity effect in multimedia learning. *Computers & Education*, *49*(4), 1147-1160. doi:10.1016/j.compedu.2006.01.008

Fidler, F., (2006). Should Psychology abandon p values and teach CIs instead? Evidence-based reforms in statistics education. In *Proceedings of the seventh international conference on teaching statistics*. International Association for Statistical Education.

Finch, S. (1998). Explaining the law of large numbers. In *Proceedings of the fifth international conference on teaching statistics* (pp. 731-736). Retrieved from: https://www.stat.auckland.ac.nz/~iase/publications/2/Topic6n.pdf

Garfield, J., & Ben-Zvi, D. (2007). How students learn statistics revisited: A current review of research on teaching and learning statistics. *International Statistical Review*, *75*(3), 372-396. doi:10.1111/j.1751-5823.2007.00029.x

Garfield, J., delMas, B., Chance, B., Poly, C., & Ooms, A. (2006). ARTIST Scale: Confidence Intervals, One-Sample [Questionnaire]. Unpublished instrument. Retrieved by mail contact.

Gigerenzer, G., Krauss, S., & Vitouch, O. (2004). The null ritual. *The Sage handbook of quantitative methodology for the social sciences*, 391-408. Retrieved from: http://www.sozialpsychologie.uni-frankfurt.de/wp-content/uploads/2010/09/GG_Null_20042.pdf

Gliner, J. A., Leech, N. L., & Morgan, G. A. (2002). Problems with null hypothesis significance testing (NHST): What do the textbooks say? *The Journal of Experimental Education*, *71*(1), 83–92. Retrieved from: http://www.andrews.edu/~rbailey/ Chapter%20two/7217331.pdf

Haller, H., & Krauss, S. (2002). Misinterpretations of significance: A problem students share with their teachers? *Methods of Psychological Research*, *7*(1), 1–20. Retrieved from: http://www2.uni-jena.de/svw/metheval/lehre/0405-ws/evaluationuebung/haller.pdf

Hulshof, C. D., Eysink, T. H., Loyens, S., & De Jong, T. (2005). *Interactive Learning Environments*, *13*(1-2), 39-53. Retrieved from: http://hal.archives-ouvertes.fr/docs/00/19/06/87/PDF/Hulshof-Casper-2005.pdf

Jazayeri, M., Lai, J., Fidler, F., & Cumming, G. (2010) Understanding of sampling variability: Confronting students'misconception in relation to sampling variability. Retrieved from: http://opax.swin.edu.au/~3420701/OZCOTS2010/OZCOTS2010_paper_Jazayeri%20et%20al.pdf

Kalinowski, P., Fidler, F., & Cumming, G. (2008). Overcoming the Inverse Probability Fallacy. *Methodology: European Journal of Research Methods for the Behavioral and Social Sciences*, *4*(4), 152-158. doi: 10.1027/1614-2241.4.4.152

Kirk, R. E. (2001). Promoting good statistical practices: Some suggestions. *Educational and Psychological Measurement*, *61*(2), 213-218. doi: 10.1177/00131640121971185

Kuhn, D., & Dean, D. (2005). Is developing scientific thinking all about learning to control variables?. *Psychological Science*, *16*(11), 866-870. Retrieved from: http://www.mx1.educationforthinking.org/sites/default/files/pdf/04%20%20Is%20Developing%20all%20about%20learning%20to%20control%20variables%20DeanAndKuhn_2005.pdf

Leonhart, R., Schornstein, K., & Lichtenberg, S. (2004). *Lehrbuch Statistik* (1st ed.). H. Huber.

Limón, M. (2001). On the cognitive conflict as an instructional strategy for conceptual change: A critical appraisal. *Learning and instruction*, *11*(4), 357-380. Retrieved from: http://www.researchgate.net/publication/236272153_1.1.cognitive_conflict/file/9c9605178181e96176.pdf

Lipson, K. (2002). The role of computer based technology in developing understanding of the concept of sampling distribution. In *Proceedings of the Sixth International Conference on Teaching of Statistics, Cape Town. Voorburg, The Netherlands: International Statistical Institute*. Retrieved from: http://www.stat.auckland.ac.nz/~iase/publications/1/6c1_lips.pdf

Liu, T.-C. (2010). Developing Simulation-based Computer Assisted Learning to Correct Students' Statistical Misconceptions based on Cognitive Conflict Theory, using "Correlation" as an Example. *Educational Technology & Society*, *13*(2), 180–192. Retrieved from: http://www.ifets.info/journals/13_2/ets_13_2.pdf

Martin, V. L., & Pressley, M. (1991). Elaborative-interrogation effects depend on the nature of the question. *Journal of Educational Psychology*, *83*(1), 113-119. doi: 10.1037/0022-0663.83.1.113

Mayer, R. E. (2005). Cognitive theory of multimedia learning. *The Cambridge handbook of multimedia learning*, 31-48. Retrieved from: http://files.onearmedman.com/fordham/mayer2005ch3.pdf

Mayer, R. E. (2011). Instruction based on visualizations. *Handbook of research on learning and instruction*, 427-445. Retrieved from: http://xa.yimg.com/kq/groups/22835952/951217969/name/__Handbook_of_Research_on_Learning_and_Instruction.pdf#page=442

Mayer, R. E., & Moreno, R. (1998). A cognitive theory of multimedia learning: Implications for design principles. In *annual meeting of the ACM SIGCHI Conference on*

Human Factors in Computing Systems, Los Angeles, CA. Retrieved from: http://spnd423.com/ SPND%20423%20Readings/A%20Cognitive%20Theory.pdf

Moreno, R., & Mayer, R. E. (2005). Role of Guidance, Reflection, and Interactivity in an Agent-Based Multimedia Game. *Journal of educational psychology, 97*(1), 117-128. doi: 10.1037/0022-0663.97.1.117

Reichheld, F. F. (2003). The one number you need to grow. *Harvard business review, 81*(12), 46-55. Retrieved from: http://www.thedatashop.co.uk/docs/NetPromoter Score_ HBR.pdf

Renkl, A. (2005). The worked-out-example principle in multimedia learning. *The Cambridge handbook of multimedia learning*, 229-245.

Renkl, A. (2013). Toward an Instructionally Oriented Theory of Example-Based Learning. *Cognitive science. 38*(1), 1-37. doi: 10.1111/cogs.12086

Rey, G. D. (2009). *E-Learning: Theorien, Gestaltungsempfehlungen und Forschung* (1st ed.). Bern: Hans Huber.

Saldanha, L., & Thompson, P. (2007). Exploring connections between sampling distributions and statistical inference: An analysis of students' engagement and thinking in the context of instruction involving repeated sampling. In *International Electronic Journal of Mathematics Education, 2(3),* 270-297. Retrieved from: http://citeseerx.ist.psu.edu/viewdoc/download?doi=10.1.1.122.9257&rep=rep1&typ e=pdf

Salden, R., Koedinger, K. R., Renkl, A., Aleven, V., & McLaren, B. M. (2010). Accounting for beneficial effects of worked examples in tutored problem solving. *Educational Psychology Review, 22*, 379–392.
Retrieved from: https://www.cs.cmu.edu/afs/cs.cmu.edu/Web/People/bmclaren/ pubs/SaldenEtAl-BeneficialEffectsWorkedExamplesinTutoredProbSolving-EdPsych Rev2010.pdf

Schwartz, D. L., & Martin, T. (2004). Inventing to prepare for future learning: The hidden efficiency of encouraging original student production in statistics instruction. *Cognition and Instruction, 22*(2), 129-184. Retrieved from: http://aaalab.stanford.edu/ papers/CI2202pp129-184.pdf

Sedlmeier, P. (1998). The distribution matters: two types of sample-size tasks. *Journal of Behavioral Decision Making, 11*(4), 281-301. Retrieved from: http://onlinelibrary. wiley.com/doi/10.1002/(SICI)1099-0771(1998120)11:4%3C281::AID-BDM302 %3E3.0.CO;2-U/pdf

Seifert, T. L. (1993). Effects of elaborative interrogation with prose passages. *Journal of Educational Psychology, 85*(4), 642-651. Retrieved from: http://scholar.google.ch/ scholar?q=info:nLdhMl2SuhwJ:scholar.google.com/&output=instlink&hl=en&as_ sdt=0,5&scillfp=12573446637631903850&oi=lle

Shaughnessy, J. M., & Ciancetta, M. (2002). Students' understanding of variability in a probability environment. In *Proceedings of the Sixth International Conference on Teaching Statistics.*Sweller, 1994. Retrieved from: http://iase-web.org/documents/ papers/icots6/6a6_shau.pdf

Sweller, J. (1994). Cognitive load theory, learning difficulty, and instructional design. *Learning and instruction, 4*(4), 295-312. Retrieved from: http://coral.ufsm.br/ tielletcab/Apostilas/cognitive_load_theory_sweller.pdf

Sweller, J., Van Merriënboer, J. J., & Paas, F. G. (1998). Cognitive architecture and instructional design. *Educational psychology review*, *10*(3), 251-296. Retrieved from: http://www.davidlewisphd.com/courses/EDD8121/readings/1998-Sweller_et_al.pdf

Trey, L., & Kahn, S. (2008). How science students can learn about unobservable phenomena using computer-based analogies. *Computers & Education*, *51*, 519–529. doi:10.1016/j.compedu.2007.05.019

Watson, J. M., & Moritz, J. B. (2000). Development of understanding of sampling for statistical literacy. *The Journal of Mathematical Behavior*, *19*(1), 109-136. Retrieved from: http://www.sciencedirect.com/science/article/pii/S0732312300000390

Well, A. D., Pollatsek, A., & Boyce, S. J. (1990). Understanding the effects of sample size on the variability of the mean. *Organizational Behavior and Human Decision Processes*, *47*(2), 289-312. doi: 10.1016/0749-5978(90)90040-G

Willoughby, T., Waller, T., Wood, E., & MacKinnon, G. E. (1993). The effect of prior knowledge on an immediate and delayed associative learning task following elaborative interrogation. *Contemporary Educational Psychology*, *18*(1), 36-46. doi: 10.1006/ceps.1993.1005

Woloshyn, V. E., Paivio, A., & Pressley, M. (1994). Use of elaborative interrogation to help students acquire information consistent with prior knowledge and information inconsistent with prior knowledge. *Journal of Educational Psychology*, *86*(1), 79-89. doi: 10.1037/0022-0663.86.1.79

Wood, E., Pressley, M., & Winne, P. H. (1990). Elaborative interrogation effects on children's learning of factual content. *Journal of Educational Psychology*, *82*(4), 741-748. doi: 10.1037/0022-0663.82.4.741

Appendix

Appendix A

Learning goals of the tutorial Statisticum

The learning environment Statisticum was created according to two main goals and seven subgoals. These goals were predefined in discussion and applied in the learning tasks of the web prototype. Module 3 was planned in order to explain statistical significance but was not assessed in this study because the program was not finished at the start of data collection.

Table A
Learning goals of the online tutorial Statisticum.

Goals of Module 1

1. Understand and read the *distribution of raw data* on the abscissa or x-axis
2. Understand and read data in *absolute* and *relative frequency* and *density histograms*
3. Understand the effect of the *interval width* on data representation in these three types of histogram.
4. Understand the concepts *probability distribution* and the *normal distribution* in relation to data.

Goals of Module 2

1. Understand the *sampling distribution* of the *mean* and its relation to the *distribution of a sample* (also called measurements distribution)
2. Understand the effects of changes in statistical characteristics (sample size N and *amount of samples*) on the *sampling distribution*.
3. Understand the meaning of the *confidence interval*.

Goals of Module 3

1. Understand construction of the *p-value*.
2. Get to know the *t-distribution* as a sampling distribution and understand the influence of N on the *t-distribution*.
3. Understand the effects of N and *SD* on the *t value*.
4. Understand the meaning of the *null hypothesis* and the relation between the distribution under H_0 and μ_0.
5. Understand the *p-value* and the *level of significance*.

Appendix B

Detailed scoring for pretest, immediate post-test and delayed post-test

To determine scores in the knowledge and understanding test about statistics the following score levels were used.

Table B 1
Scoring table for items 1 to 7.

Test item	Question type	Question goal	Possible answers	Scoring
Item 1	Open-ended	Reading and interpreting data	No answer or incorrect Incomplete answer Partly correct Correct	0 0 0.5 1.0
Item 2	Open-ended	Reading and interpreting data	No answer or incorrect Incomplete answer Partly correct Correct	0 0 0.5 1.0
Item 3	Open-ended	Reading and interpreting data	No answer or incorrect Partly correct Answer is the same as in Item 2 Correct	0 0.5 0.5 1.0
Item 4	Open-ended	Predict changes of a statistical parameter	No answer or incorrect Partly correct Correct	0 0.5 1.0
Item 5	Open-ended	Reading and interpreting data	No answer or incorrect Partly correct Correct	0 0.5 1.0
Item 6	Open-ended	Predict changes of a statistical parameter	No answer or incorrect Plausible range Plausible range and plausible values	0 0.5 1.0

Item 7	Open-ended	Predict changes of a statistical parameter	No answer or incorrect (with or without reasoning)	0
			Correct answer (with incorrect reasoning or without reasoning)	0.5
			Correct answer and correct reasoning	1.0

Table B 2

Scoring table for items 8 to 11.

Test item	Question type	Question goal	Possible answers	Scoring
Item 8	Multiple choice	Understand relation between distribution of a sample and sampling distribution	No answer or incorrect answer Correct	0 1.0
Item 9	Multiple choice	Conceptual understanding by way of example	No answer or incorrect Correct	0 1.0
Item 10 a), b), c)	Open-ended	Predict changes of a statistical parameter	No answer or incorrect Correct	0 1.0
Item 11	Multiple choice	Conceptual understanding by way of example	No answer or incorrect Correct	0 1.0

Note. Item 10 was divided into three subtasks a) - c). Each subtask was rated separately with the provided scoring.

Appendix C

Detailed statistics of scores in the objective knowledge and understanding test

Table C 1

Mean scores per question for items 1 to 8.

		Measuring time point					
		Pretest		Immediate Post-test		Delayed Post-test	
Test task	Condition	*n*	*M(SD)*	*n*	*M(SD)*	*n*	*M(SD)*
1)	Dynamic	21	0.83(0.37)	21	0.95(0.15)	20	0.90(0.26)
	Static	18	1.00(0.00)	18	1.00(0.00)	18	1.00(0.00)
2)	Dynamic	21	0.45(0.27)	21	0.67(0.29)	20	0.60(0.26)
	Static	18	0.56(0.24)	18	0.67(0.24)	18	0.58(0.26)
3)	Dynamic	21	0.19(0.25)	21	0.50(0.27)	20	0.40(0.34)
	Static	18	0.22(0.26)	18	0.36(0.33)	18	0.31(0.30)
4 a)	Dynamic	21	0.67(0.24)	21	0.86(0.23)	20	0.68(0.24)
	Static	18	0.67(0.24)	18	1.00(0.00)	18	0.83(0.24)
4 b)	Dynamic	21	0.69(0.25)	21	0.85(0.23)	20	0.70(0.25)
	Static	18	0.67(0.24)	18	1.00(0.00)	18	0.81(0.25)
5)	Dynamic	21	0.00(0.00)	21	0.52(0.43)	20	0.38(0.43)
	Static	18	0.00(0.00)	18	0.56(0.42)	18	0.25(0.43)

6)	Dynamic	21	0.71(0.37)	21	0.76(0.34)	20	0.75(0.34)
	Static	18	0.67(0.38)	18	0.75(0.31)	18	0.69(0.35)
7)	Dynamic	21	0.21(0.25)	21	0.55(0.42)	20	0.53(0.37)
	Static	18	0.36(0.29)	18	0.47(0.36)	18	0.42(0.35)
8)	Dynamic	21	0.52(0.51)	21	0.62(0.50)	20	0.56(0.51)
	Static	18	0.61(0.50)	18	0.67(0.49)	18	0.55(0.51)

Note. For each question a participants could get 1 point for a correct answer and 0 point for an incorrect answer. Sometimes participants could get 0.5 points, for instance if a task demanded reasoning about the answer (for details about scoring see Appendix B).

Table C 2

Mean scores per question for items 9 to 11.

Test task	Condition	Pretest		Immediate Post-test		Delayed Post-test	
		Measuring time point					
		n	*M(SD)*	*n*	*M(SD)*	*n*	*M(SD)*
9)	Dynamic	21	0.76(0.44)	21	0.57(0.51)	20	0.55(0.51)
	Static	18	0.28(0.46)	18	0.50(0.51)	18	0.56(9.51)
10 a)	Dynamic	13	0.31(0.48)	21	0.76(0.44)	20	0.65(0.50)
	Static	10	0.70(0.48)	18	0.94(0.24)	18	0.78(0.43)
10 b)	Dynamic	13	0.38(0.51)	21	0.43(0.51)	20	0.45(0.51)
	Static	10	0.50(0.53)	18	0.56(0.51)	18	0.56(0.51)
10 c)	Dynamic	13	0.08(0.28)	21	0.48(0.51)	20	0.40(0.50)
	Static	10	0.10(0.32)	18	0.56(0.51)	18	0.67(0.49)
11)	Dynamic	13	0.38(0.51)	21	0.57(0.51)	20	0.45(0.51)
	Static	10	0.40(0.52)	18	0.50(0.51)	18	0.56(0.51)

Note. For each question a participants could get 1 point for a correct answer and 0 point for an incorrect answer. Sometimes participants could get 0.5 points, for instance if a task demanded reasoning about the answer (for details about scoring see Appendix B).

If you have any concerns about our products,
you can contact us on
ProductSafety@springernature.com

In case Publisher is established outside the EU,
the EU authorized representative is:
**Springer Nature Customer Service Center GmbH
Europaplatz 3, 69115 Heidelberg, Germany**

Printed by Libri Plureos GmbH
in Hamburg, Germany